Little Red Riding Hood

Cappuccetto Rosso

G GIUNTI Junior

This is the story of Little
Red Riding Hood.

She lives with her
mother in a
cottage near
the wood.

Her Grandmother
makes her a red cloak
with a hood.

She loves it!

She always wears
it and everyone
calls her Little
Red Riding Hood.

One day Grandmother is ill.
– Take this basket to
Grandmother but remember:
don't stop in the wood
and don't talk to any
strangers – says
Mother.

In the basket
there are some buns,
a bottle of wine
and some cakes.

So Little Red Riding Hood
leaves with the basket.

On the way she sees
hunters and woodcutters
but she remembers she
mustn't talk to strangers.

She sings
a song and she
doesn't see a big,
grey wolf.

But then she sees
him behind a tree.

The wolf jumps out in
front of her, smiling.
– Where are you going,
little girl? – he asks.

– I'm going to see my
Grandmother, who is ill –
she says.

The wolf smiles again.

– Why don't you pick some
flowers for her? – he says.

– Good idea, Mr. Wolf –
she says.

She picks lots of flowers:
red, yellow, pink, orange,
purple and blue.

There are so many
flowers... she wants
to pick them all!

The wolf runs
down the path
to find
Grandmother's
cottage.

He is very hungry.

The wolf finds the cottage.
Grandmother
is in bed.

The wolf knocks
on the door.

– Who's there? – asks
Grandmother.

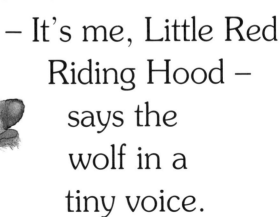

– It's me, Little Red
Riding Hood –
says the
wolf in a
tiny voice.

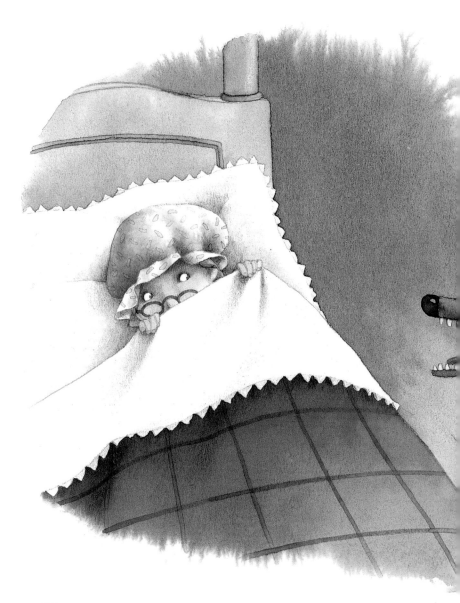

– Come in – says
Grandmother.

The wolf opens the door,
runs in and eats her up
in one big gulp.

He puts on
Grandmother's glasses
and night cap
and goes to bed.
He waits for Little Red
Riding Hood.

Little Red
Riding Hood
is on her way to
the cottage with the basket.

She arrives at the cottage
and knocks on the door.

– It's me, Grandmother –
she says.
– Come in, my dear – says
the wolf in a squeaky voice.

– Hello, Grandmother! – says Little Red Riding Hood, showing the basket of food and the flowers.

– Grandmother,
– she says – what
big eyes you've
got!

– All the better to see
you with! –
says
the wolf.

– But Grandmother, –
says the little girl – what
big ears you've got!

– All the better to hear
you with! – says the wolf.

– But Grandmother, –
she says – what long
arms you've got!

– All the
better to
hug you
with – says
the wolf.

– But Grandmother, – says
Little Red Riding Hood –
what big teeth you've got!

– All the better… to eat
you with! – growls
the wolf.

The wolf jumps
out of bed and
eats Little Red
Riding Hood up
in one big gulp.

Out in
the wood
a woodcutter
hears a scream.

He runs in and sees
the wolf fast asleep.

He kills the wolf with
his axe and cuts it open.

Little Red Riding Hood
and her Grandmother
are still alive.

– Thank you
very much! –
they say
to the
woodcutter.

Grandmother
and Little Red
Riding Hood
are now safe
and they have
a delicious
supper!

So Little Red Riding
Hood comes back home.
Mother is so happy to see
her little girl again!
– Goodnight dear! – she
says closing the window.

TRADUZIONE

INGLESE / ITALIANO

Pagina 2

This is the story of Little Red Riding Hood.

Questa è la storia di Cappuccetto Rosso.

Pagina 3

She lives with her mother in a cottage near the wood.

Vive con la mamma in una casetta vicino al bosco.

Pagina 4

Her Grandmother makes her a red cloak with a hood.

*La nonna prepara per lei una mantellina rossa
con un cappuccio.*

Pagina 5

She loves it!

Lei la adora!

Pagina 6

She always wears it and everyone calls her Little Red Riding Hood.

La indossa sempre e tutti la chiamano Cappuccetto Rosso.

Pagina 7

One day Grandmother is ill.
– Take this basket to Grandmother but remember: don't stop in the wood and don't talk to any strangers – says Mother.

Un giorno la nonna è ammalata.
– Porta questo cestino alla nonna, ma ricorda: non fermarti nel bosco e non parlare con gli sconosciuti – dice la mamma.

Pagina 8

In the basket there are some buns, a bottle of wine and some cakes.

Nel cestino ci sono delle ciambelle, una bottiglia di vino e dei dolcetti.

Pagina 9

So Little Red Riding Hood leaves with the basket.

Così Cappuccetto Rosso parte con il cestino.

Pagina 10

On the way she sees hunters and woodcutters but she remembers she mustn't talk to strangers.

Lungo la strada vede cacciatori e taglialegna ma si ricorda che non deve parlare con gli sconosciuti.

Pagina 11

She sings a song and she doesn't see a big, grey wolf.
Canta una canzone e non vede un grande lupo grigio.

Pagina 12

But then she sees him behind a tree.

Ma poi lo vede dietro a un albero.

Pagina 13

The wolf jumps out in front of her, smiling.
– Where are you going, little girl? – he asks.

Il lupo salta fuori di fronte a lei sorridendo.
– Dove stai andando, bambina? – chiede.

Pagina 14-15

– I'm going to see my Grandmother, who is ill – she says.
The wolf smiles again.

– Sto andando a trovare la nonna che è ammalata – dice lei.
Il lupo sorride di nuovo.

Pagina 16

– Why don't you pick some flowers for her? – he says.

– Perché non raccogli dei fiori per lei? – dice.

Pagina 17

– Good idea, Mr. Wolf – she says.

– Buona idea, signor Lupo – replica lei.

Pagina 18

She picks lots of flowers: red, yellow, pink, orange, purple
and blue.

Raccoglie tanti fiori: rossi, gialli, rosa, arancioni, viola e blu.

Pagina 19

There are so many flowers... she wants to pick them all!

Ci sono così tanti fiori... che vuole raccoglierli tutti!

Pagina 20

The wolf runs down the path to find Grandmother's cottage.

Il lupo si affretta lungo il sentiero per cercare la casetta della nonna.

Pagina 21

He is very hungry.

Ha molta fame.

Pagina 22

The wolf finds the cottage.
Grandmother is in bed.

Il lupo trova la casetta.
La nonna è a letto.

Pagina 23

The wolf knocks on the door.
– Who's there? – asks Grandmother.
– It's me, Little Red Riding Hood – says the wolf in a tiny voice.

Il lupo bussa alla porta.
– Chi è? – chiede la nonna.
– Sono io, Cappuccetto Rosso – dice il lupo con una vocina tenue.

Pagina 24

– Come in – says Grandmother.

– Entra – dice la nonna.

Pagina 25

The wolf opens the door, runs in and eats her up
in one big gulp.

*Il lupo apre la porta, corre dentro e la mangia
in un sol boccone.*

Pagina 26

He puts on Grandmother's glasses and night cap and goes
to bed. He waits for Little Red Riding Hood.

*Si mette gli occhiali e la cuffia da notte della nonna e va
a letto. Aspetta Cappuccetto Rosso.*

Pagina 27

Little Red Riding Hood is on her way to the cottage
with the basket.

Cappuccetto Rosso sta arrivando alla casetta con il cestino.

Pagina 28

She arrives at the cottage and knocks on the door.

Arriva alla casetta e bussa alla porta.

Pagina 29

– It's me, Grandmother – she says.
– Come in, my dear – says the wolf in a squeaky voice.

– Sono io, nonna – esclama.
– Entra, mia cara – dice il lupo con una vocina stridula.

Pagina 30
– Hello, Grandmother! – says Little Red Riding Hood, showing the basket of food and the flowers.

– Ciao, nonna! – dice Cappuccetto Rosso, mostrando
il cestino del cibo e i fiori.

Pagina 31
– Grandmother, – she says – what big eyes you've got!
– All the better to see you with! – says the wolf.

– Nonna, – dice – che occhi grandi hai!
– Per guardarti meglio! – dice il lupo.

Pagina 32
– But Grandmother, – says the little girl – what big ears you've got!

– Ma nonna, – dice la bambina – che orecchie grandi hai!

Pagina 33
– All the better to hear you with! – says the wolf.

– Per sentirti meglio! – dice il lupo.

Pagina 34
– But Grandmother, – she says – what long arms you've got!
– All the better to hug you with! – says the wolf.

– Ma nonna, – esclama – che braccia lunghe hai!
– Per abbracciarti meglio! – dice il lupo.

Pagina 35
– But Grandmother, – says Little Red Riding Hood – what big teeth you've got!
– All the better... to eat you with! – growls the wolf.

– Ma nonna, – dice Cappuccetto Rosso – che denti grandi hai!
– Per... mangiarti meglio! – ringhia il lupo.

Pagine 36-37
The wolf jumps out of bed and eats Little Red Riding Hood up in one big gulp.

Il lupo salta fuori dal letto e mangia Cappuccetto Rosso in sol boccone.

Pagine 38
Out in the wood a woodcutter hears a scream.

Fuori nel bosco un taglialegna sente un urlo.

Pagina 39
He runs in and sees the wolf fast asleep.

Corre dentro e vede il lupo addormentato.

Pagina 40
He kills the wolf with his axe and cuts it open.

Uccide il lupo con la sua ascia e gli apre la pancia.

Pagina 41
Little Red Riding Hood and her Grandmother are still alive.
– Thank you very much! – they say to the woodcutter.

Cappuccetto Rosso e la nonna sono ancora vive.
– Grazie mille! – dicono al taglialegna.

Pagine 42-43

Grandmother and Little Red Riding Hood are now safe
and they have a delicious supper!

La nonna e Cappuccetto Rosso ora sono salve
e festeggiano con una deliziosa cenetta!

Pagine 44-45

So Little Red Riding Hood comes back home.
Mother is so happy to see her little girl again!
– Goodnight dear! – she says closing the window.

Così Cappuccetto Rosso torna a casa.
La mamma è così felice di vedere di nuovo la sua bambina!
– Buonanotte, tesoro! – dice chiudendo la finestra.

Short summary

 lives in a  with
her .

One day she has to go and
see her who is ill.
On the way she meets a .
He tells her to pick some
 and runs to find
Grandmother's cottage.
He eats her up in one big
gulp and goes to .

When Little Red Riding Hood
arrives, she thinks
Grandmother looks strange.
But the wolf eats her up in
one big gulp.
Then a comes.
He kills the wolf and saves
Grandmother and Little Red
Riding Hood.

Find the Differences

Look carefully at the two pictures
and find the 5 differences.

*Osserva attentamente le due immagini
e trova le 5 differenze.*

A Wordsearch

Find 4 words of the story!

Trova 4 parole della storia!

WOLF   **COTTAGE**

MOTHER   **WOOD**

Q	H	C	S	R	C
D	W	O	L	F	I
B	W	T	S	V	O
M	O	T	H	E	R
A	O	A	Z	N	C
I	D	G	F	G	A
F	M	E	L	P	U

What is this?
Join the numbers from one to eighteen!

Unisci i numeri dall'uno al diciotto!

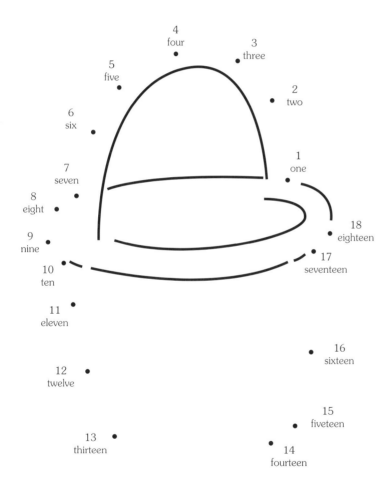

4 four

3 three

5 five

2 two

6 six

1 one

7 seven

8 eight

18 eighteen

9 nine

17 seventeen

10 ten

11 eleven

16 sixteen

12 twelve

15 fifteen

13 thirteen

14 fourteen

THIS IS THE LITTLE RED RIDING HOOD'S **B** _ _ _ _ _ _ !

Match the Word with the picture!

*Unisci parole
e immagini!*

GRANDMOTHER

LITTLE RED
RIDING HOOD

WOLF

MOTHER

A Crossword

Risolvi
il cruciverba
illustrato!

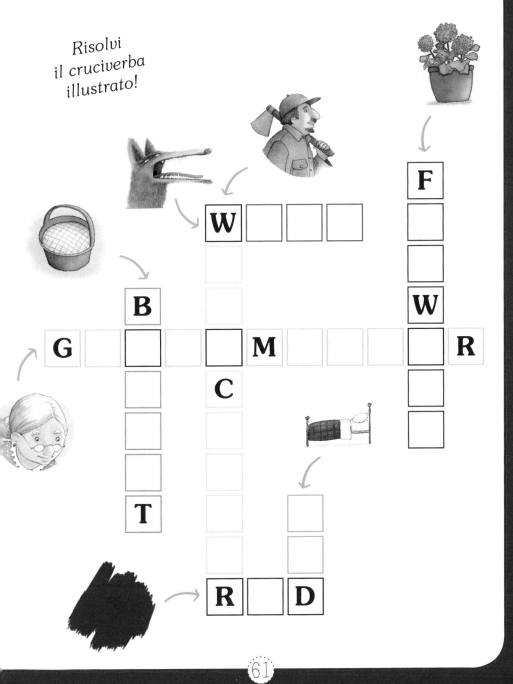

A Maze
Help Little Red Riding Hood
to reach her Grandmother's cottage!

*Aiuta Cappuccetto Rosso a raggiungere
la casetta della nonna!*

A little dictionary

ARM: BRACCIO

BASKET: CESTINO

BED: LETTO

CAKE: TORTA

DOOR: PORTA

EAR: ORECCHIO

EYE: OCCHIO

FLOWER: FIORE

GRANDMOTHER: NONNA

HOOD: CAPPUCCIO

HUNTER: CACCIATORE

MOTHER: MADRE

PATH: SENTIERO

SCREAM: URLO

TOOTH/TEETH: DENTE/DENTI

TREE: ALBERO

WOLF: LUPO

WOOD: BOSCO

WOODCUTTER: TAGLIALEGNA

BIG: GRANDE • • • **aggettivi** • • •

HUNGRY: AFFAMATO

ILL: MALATO

LITTLE: PICCOLO

RED: ROSSO

to EAT: MANGIARE

to FIND: TROVARE

to HEAR: SENTIRE

to HUG: ABBRACCIARE

to JUMP: SALTARE

to KILL: UCCIDERE

to KNOCK: BUSSARE

to LOVE: AMARE, ADORARE

to OPEN: APRIRE

to PICK: COGLIERE

to SEE: VEDERE

to SMILE: SORRIDERE

to WEAR: INDOSSARE

• • • **verbi** • • •

A cura di Gabriella Ballarin
Illustrazioni: Valentina Salmaso
Progetto grafico
e impaginazione: Simonetta Zuddas

www.giunti.it

© 2010, 2016 Giunti Editore S.p.A.
Via Bolognese, 165 - 50139 Firenze - Italia
Piazza Virgilio, 4 - 20123 Milano - Italia

Prima edizione: maggio 2006
Prima edizione con CD: settembre 2010

MISTO
Carta da fonti gestite
in maniera responsabile
FSC® C016466
FSC
www.fsc.org

Stampato presso Lito Terrazzi srl, stabilimento di Iolo